FIRE SAFETY

Crawl Low under Smoke

by Lucia Raatma

Bridgestone Books
an imprint of Capstone Press
Mankato, Minnesota

Bridgestone Books are published by Capstone Press
818 North Willow Street, Mankato, Minnesota 56001
http://www.capstone-press.com

Library of Congress Cataloging-in-Publication Data
Raatma, Lucia.
    Crawl low under smoke/by Lucia Raatma.
    p. cm.—(Fire safety)
    Includes bibliographical references and index.
    Summary: Explains how to leave a building safely during a fire, emphasizing
staying low to avoid smoke and using alternate ways out.
    ISBN 0-7368-0194-4
    1. Fires—Safety measures—Juvenile literature. [1. Fires. 2. Safety.] I. Title. II. Series:
Raatma, Lucia. Fire safety.
TH9148.R3 1999
628.9'2—DC21
                                                                              98-46538
                                                                                   CIP
                                                                                    AC

Editorial Credits
Rebecca Glaser, editor; Timothy Halldin, cover designer and illustrator; Kimberly
  Danger, photo researcher

Photo Credits
Gregg R. Andersen, cover, 6, 8, 10, 12, 14, 16, 18, 20
Shaffer Photography/James L. Shaffer, 4

Capstone Press would like to thank George A. Miller, Chief of Fire Code Enforcement,
New Jersey Division of Fire Safety, for reviewing this material.

Table of Contents

Fires

Fires are dangerous. Fires can make
a lot of smoke. Fire and smoke can
spread quickly through buildings. You
must be prepared to escape in case of a
fire. Escaping quickly is the best way
to stay safe.

The Danger of Smoke

Smoke is a dangerous part of fire. Smoky air is hard to breathe. Breathing smoke makes people sick. You should crawl low under smoke. The air is not as smoky near the floor.

Smoke Alarms

Smoke alarms warn people of smoke and fire. These machines make a loud noise when they sense smoke. Go outside quickly if you hear a smoke alarm. Crawl low if there is smoke.

Know Where to Go

You and your family should plan an escape route from your home. Find two ways to leave each room. Choose a place for your family to meet outside. Practicing an escape route will help you know where to go during a fire.

escape route

a planned way to leave your home

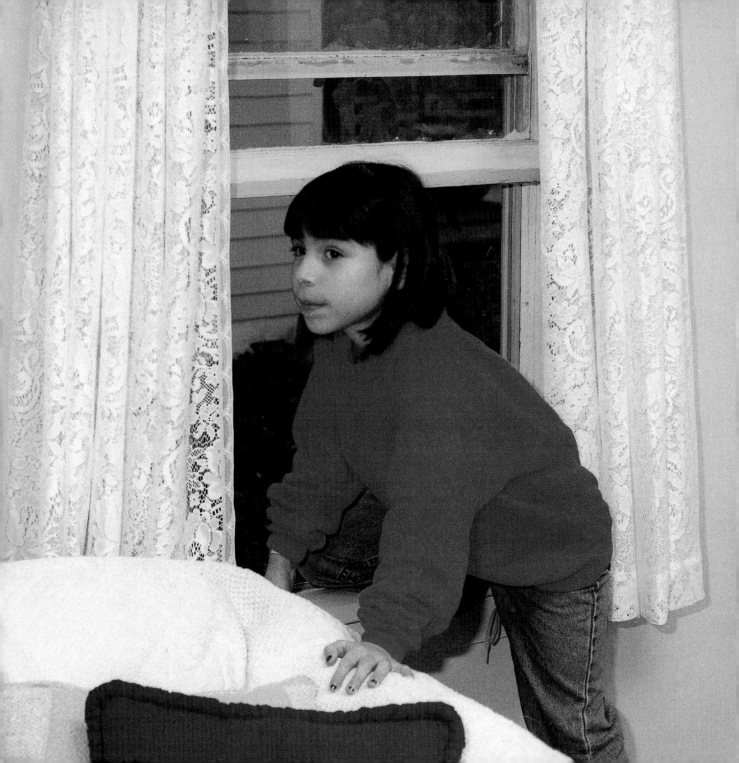

Two Ways Out

Try first to leave through a door when a smoke alarm sounds. Quickly touch a closed door. If the door feels cool, open it slowly. A hot door means that fire or smoke could be on the other side. If the door feels hot, leave through another exit such as a window.

exit

a way out of a building

Crawl Low

You may have to go through smoke to get to your exit. Smoke rises to the top of a room. The best way to avoid smoke is to crawl low. Crawl on your hands and knees. Stay under the smoke. The air near the floor is easier to breathe.

Safety in Apartment Buildings

Apartment buildings should have signs that mark fire exits. During a fire, use the closest exit. Always take the stairs. Never use an elevator during a fire. The fire may cause the elevator to break. Do not enter a smoke-filled hallway or stairs. Use your second way out.

Staying Outside

The first person to escape from a fire should call the fire department. Wait outside for the firefighters to arrive. Never go back into a burning building. You could get hurt. Tell firefighters if anyone is still inside. Then stay back and let the firefighters work.

Be Prepared

Fire and smoke are dangerous. They can hurt you. But you can get out safely if you are prepared. Talk to your family and friends about fire safety. Tell them why smoke is dangerous. Show them how to crawl low and stay under smoke.

Hands On: Crawling Low

Crawling below the smoke is important when escaping fire. You can practice crawling low with this activity.

<u>What You Need</u>
Classmates, friends, or family
An adult to watch
A long stick or broom handle

<u>What You Do</u>
1. Have two people each hold one end of the stick.
2. Hold the stick at about five feet (1.5 meters) above the ground.
3. Pretend the stick is smoke. Take turns going under the stick. Walk quickly as you would if escaping from a fire.
4. Have the two people hold the stick about two feet (.6 meter) off the ground.
5. Take turns going under the stick again. Crawl on your hands and knees under the stick. Who can crawl the fastest?

Words to Know

avoid (uh-VOID)—to stay away from something

escape (ess-KAPE)—to get away from something

escape route (ess-KAPE ROOT)—a planned way to leave your home; escape routes include two ways out of each room and a meeting place outside.

exit (EG-zit)—a way out of a building

smoke alarm (SMOHK uh-LARM)—a machine that warns people of smoke by making a loud sound

Read More

Butler, Daphne. *What Happens when Fire Burns*. What Happens When... Austin, Tex.: Raintree Steck-Vaughn, 1996.

Loewen, Nancy. *Fire Safety*. Plymouth, Minn.: Child's World, 1997.

Raatma, Lucia. *Safety around Fire*. Safety First! Mankato, Minn.: Bridgestone Books, 1999.

Internet Sites

Sparky's Home Page
http://www.sparky.org/
United States Fire Administration (USFA) Kids Homepage
http://www.usfa.fema.gov/kids/index.htm

Index